Zoe' Lemonade Stand

Kid Business Workbook

"When Life Gives You Lemons, Make Lemonade!"

By Zoe' Howlett

Biography

Zoe Howlett is a trailblazing Entrepreneur, Author, and Philanthropist who began her journey at just six years old. Amid her family's struggles with homelessness, Zoe' started a lemonade stand that quickly became a success, grossing over $5,000 per month. Her entrepreneurial spirit didn't stop there Zoe went on to self-publish two kid business workbooks, empowering young minds to explore entrepreneurship.

During the COVID-19 pandemic, Zoe made a profound impact on her community by purchasing and donating over 6,000 books to children without access to libraries. She also organized community movie nights, giving kids a safe and fun way to socialize during the lockdown.

Now, Zoe inspires the next generation of leaders by hosting children's business fairs, where she promotes hands-on business experience, customer engagement and money management, that uplifts young entrepreneurs. Zoe's journey is a powerful example of how community support, determination and mentorship can transform challenges into opportunities to uplift future generations.

Zoe' Howlett
CEO

This Workbook Belongs To:

_____

Dedication

This book is dedicated to you the bold, brilliant young entrepreneurs who dare to dream big and work hard. May you pursue your dreams with passion, resilience, and integrity.

Remember, the path to success is not always straight, but with hard work, dedication, and an unwavering belief in yourself, you can accomplish anything you set your mind to.

May your journey be fulfilling, your hearts be full, and your minds stay forever curious. I believe in you, and I am endlessly proud of the incredible leader and change-maker you are destined to become.

We believe in you. We are proud of you. The future is yours to build.

With love,
Zoe' and The Lemonade Stand Family

Table of Contents

Special Message

Entrepreneurship Starts With You

Hobbies and Interest....................1

Becoming an Entrepreneur..........3

Business Start Up..............................10

Growing Your Business................14

Business Goals Setting.................16

Business Overview.........................18

Marketing Tips...............................19

Customer Service Tips..................20

Tips On Customer Complaints.....21

Business Glossary.........................22

Meet the Creator

Bonus Sheets

Special Message

What do you want to be when you grow up?

How many times have your parents or other adults asked you that question? It probably feels like adults are always asking kids what they want to be when they get older. But there's a good reason for it, they want you to start thinking about your future!

Different careers require different skills, and your parents want to make sure you have everything you need to succeed. If you want to be a doctor, for example, you'll need to go to medical school. If you want to be an artist, you might study fine arts. Some of you might already know what you want to be, and some of you might not and guess what? That's okay! You've got plenty of time to figure it out.

That's what this book is all about: helping you start planning for your future right now. And one of the most important things to learn early is how money, budgeting, and saving work in the grown-up world.

This workbook will help you learn, plan, and dream bigger and it will even show you fun ways you can start saving and earning your own money right now!

Get ready to begin your exciting journey!

Entrepreneurship Starts With You

Starting your own business is exciting, fun and can be very rewarding. As you begin your journey into being a kid entrepreneur, there are a few important things to remember.

- Overnight success is rare
- You must surround yourself with other like-minded kids, entrepreneurs and adults.
- Believe in your ideas
- Be consistent

According to the National Financial Educators Council "20 percent of parents say students aren't prepared to deal with the financial challenges that await them in the real world." Ultimately, this can result in varying degrees of financial difficulties from at minimum some bumps in the road to extreme debt on the other side of the scale.

In addition, no matter what career path you take, having an entrepreneurial attitude will serve you well.

Reference MLA: www.nationalfinancialeducatorscouncil.com

HOBBIES AND INTEREST

What are some of your hobbies and interests?

1._____

2._____

3._____

4._____

5._____

What type of businesses could you create from your hobbies and interests?

1._____

2._____

3._____

4._____

5._____

Of the business ideas you listed above, which one do you think could be a business for you?

1._____

2._____

3._____

4._____

5._____

HOBBIES AND INTEREST

What other options do people have for what you provide? Are there any other kids in your area with the same business idea?

1._____

2._____

3._____

4._____

5._____

In what ways have your parents supported and guided you in sports, activities or a cool idea.

1._____

2._____

3._____

4._____

5._____

Moziah Bridges

Founded Mo's Bows, a bow tie business, at the age of 9. In 2016, Moziah was on Fortune's "18 under 18" list of the country's most innovative and ambitious teens. By 2017, the National Basketball Association sealed a partnership with the young fashion designer to make custom neckties and bow ties for all 30 NBA teams.

BECOMING AN ENTREPRENEUR

An entrepreneur is someone who owns his or her own business. You will be responsible for the hours you work.

Write out the hours you think you will work your business.

_____

Who is your "target market"?

A target market is the group of people who are most likely to buy products from you. Describe your ideal customer below.

_____

_____

_____

_____

_____

What will make your business stand out from someone else?

_____

_____

_____

_____

_____

So what do you think? Do you think you have what it takes to be an entrepreneur?

Write your thoughts below and brainstorm your business idea.

_____

_____

_____

_____

_____

_____

_____

_____

_____

_____

BECOMING AN ENTREPRENEUR

It's time for you to test out the idea you came up with. It's important to make sure people have a need for what you're offering, and more importantly, if they are willing to spend their money with you.

Think again about who you think your target audience is and how your business will help them. Ask yourself what you think people would be willing to pay for what you want to offer.

Describe your idea in detail below and what will be your business name.

_____

_____

_____

_____

_____

_____

_____

_____

_____

_____

What need does your product or service fill? What problem are you solving for people who buy from you?

_____

_____

_____

_____

_____

How much do you plan to sell your product or service for?

_____

_____

_____

_____

_____

List 5 - 8 words that describe what your business does.

_____

_____

_____

_____

_____

List several words that describe a benefit of your product or service.

What words can you think of that are catchy and memorable even if they aren't real words?

_____

_____

_____

_____

_____

Time to test out your business name idea.

_____

_____

_____

_____

Let's get some feedback on your business name idea. Many entrepreneurs choose company names that include their own name or the city or state where they live. Whether this is a good idea for your business or not depends on what your business is and what you hope to accomplish in the future.

List several name ideas for your business below:

_____

_____

_____

_____

BECOMING AN ENTREPRENEUR

Once you have a few business name ideas, present them to your family, friends, neighbors and get their feedback. Make sure you write down and circle the best name and number them 1, 2, and 3.

1. _____

2. _____

3. _____

4. _____

5. _____

BUSINESS START-UP

Who will be investing in your business idea?

Most small startup businesses get family and friends to invest in their business. You can get a small business loan for start-up costs as well. No matter who you approach for an investment in your business idea, it's important to be honest, professional and prepared for a possible no.

Name some family and friends that can invest in your business.
List below:

1._____

2._____

3._____

4._____

5._____

How much money do you think you need to start up your business?

_____

_____

_____

_____

_____

_____

BUSINESS START-UP

What exactly will you use the startup money for? Provide details about how your investor's money will be used. Be sure to account for the total amount you're asking for.

_____

_____

_____

_____

_____

_____

_____

_____

Write out how much you think your business expense cost will be.

_____

_____

_____

_____

_____

_____

Tracking your expenses and profit does not have to be difficult. It's really just a matter of listing everything you spend money on for your business. Keep track of the money coming in and the money going out, and you'll always know where you stand financially.

What are some things you'll have to buy to start your business?

_____   _____

_____   _____

_____   _____

_____   _____

_____   _____

Finding customers for your business

You know that every business needs customers right? Most new business owners don't know how to get those customers to notice their new business. You will have to choose a method to market your business, you have to know where to find your customers and how to communicate your business message. Knowing who your target market will help you identify who your clientele is, and knowing more about them.

Write out how much you think your business expense cost will be.

_____   _____

_____   _____

_____   _____

BUSINESS START-UP

Where are the people in your target market likely to spend their money?

_____

_____

_____

_____

_____

What do the people in your target market like to spend money on?

_____

_____

_____

_____

_____

Which websites are you likely to use to do research?

_____

_____

_____

_____

_____

GROWING YOUR BUSINESS

What does business growth mean to you?

_____

_____

_____

_____

_____

Would you be interested in expanding your business into other cities?

_____

_____

Where would you expand your business to if you could? Why?

_____

_____

If you could expand your business by adding more services or products, what would you add? Why?

_____

_____

Time to make it happen

We have covered a lot of information in this book. It can be very overwhelming and might seem like a-lot but it's worth learning. If you take it step by step and follow the process in this workbook, you'll have the knowledge you need to start a small business of your own.

Hold Tight! You're on the way to becoming a successful entrepreneur!

What is one important lesson you learned about starting your own business?

_____

_____

_____

How will it help you become a successful entrepreneur?

_____

_____

_____

_____

_____

_____

What is three goals you'd like to achieve for your new business in the next 3-6 months?

1. _____

2. _____

3. _____

Break this goal into at least 5 smaller goals you'll need to reach in order to achieve your business goal.

_____

_____

_____

_____

Assign a date to each goal, by which you will achieve that goal.

_____

_____

_____

_____

BUSINESS GOALS

What obstacles might you encounter on your way to your goal?

1. _____

2. _____

3. _____

4. _____

How will you overcome these obstacles?

_____

_____

_____

_____

_____

_____

Who can support you with overcoming these obstacles?

_____

_____

_____

BUSINESS OVERVIEW

Business Name: _____

Business Description: _____

Business Location: _____

Business Structure: _____

Owners Name: _____

Age: _____ Title: _____

Ownership% _____

Who are your customers? _____

How old are they?

_____

What area do they live in? _____

Who are your top 4 competitors in your area?

_____ _____ _____

_____

What perception do your potential customers have of them?

_____

How do their prices compare to your prices? _____

What do they do well?

_____

What weak areas do they demonstrate? _____

How will they win the battle for customers over our competition in this market?

_____

_____

_____

Marketing is something most business owners spend their whole lives learning. So marketing is something you're never finished learning. In general though, there are some tips to keep in mind when marketing, whatever methods you use.

1. **Keep it simple.** In today's fast-paced world, people don't have time to try and figure out what you're trying to say with your marketing.

2. **Consistency is key.** You can't expect to see long-term results if you put out one piece of marketing and sit back to wait for the sales to roll in. Marketing is an ongoing process that should never take a break.

3. **Be authentic.** Being authentic means your marketing is honest and real. People like to do business with companies that are honest and upfront in their marketing. High pressure sales or making false claims will definitely hurt your business in the long term.

CUSTOMER SERVICE TIPS

Customer Service Tips

1. Always be courteous and respectful.
2. Treat your customers with respect
3. Be professional.
4. Never argue with your customers.
5. Listen. If there is a problem, listen rather than being defensive.
6. Keep your commitments.
7. Always do what you say you're going to do.
8. Show appreciation.
9. Show your customers how much you appreciate them.
10. Be available. It can be very frustrating trying to track down a business owner when you need something from their business.
11. Watch what you say. Never discuss personal business in front of customers.
12. Smile. Even when you are on the phone, a smile can come through the phone.
13. Ask for feedback and reviews. Asking your customers how well you're doing for them can improve your business.
14. Go above and beyond. Doing more than a customer expects is a great way to keep a loyal customer.

Listen. When someone is upset about something. Don't interrupt the customer. Just let them vent and listen carefully to what they're saying.

Clarify. If you are not clear about anything the customer has told you, ask questions to get a better understanding. Even if you do not understand the customer's complaint, use this step to repeat back what you've heard and ensure a resolution.

Resolve. After you have listened carefully to your customer's complaint and have clarified to make sure you understand the entire issue, you should attempt to resolve the problem.

BUSINESS GLOSSARY

ACCOUNTING PERIOD: A period of time, (month, quarter, year), for which a financial statement is produced.

ACCOUNTS PAYABLE: This represents what a business owes to its suppliers and other creditors at a given point in time.

ACCOUNTS RECEIVABLE: This represents the amount due to a business by its customers at a given point in time.

AUDIT: Verification of financial records and accounting procedures generally conducted by a CPA or accounting firm or if you're really unlucky, the IRS.

BALANCE SHEET: Financial statement showing

BREAK-EVEN POINT: The point at which sales equal total costs.

CAPITAL ASSET: An asset that is purchased for long-term use such as machinery and equipment.

CASH ACCOUNTING: The simplest form of accounting in which income is considered earned when received and expenses are not taken into account until paid.

COLLATERAL: An asset that can be sold for cash and which has been pledged to a creditor to secure a future obligation. (For example, if you finance a car, it is the collateral for the loan).

CONTRACT: An agreement between two {or more) parties in which each promises to perform in some way. Contracts can be complex and should always be reviewed by an attorney. A contract may not be binding if not correctly drafted and executed.

BUSINESS GLOSSARY

DEBT FINANCING: This is financing in which you get a loan from someone or somewhere and go into debt! You are obligated to repay the money at some predetermined interest rate. assets and liabilities at a specific time.

DEPRECIATION: Decrease in the value of equipment over time. Depreciation of equipment used for business is a tax deductible expense.

DROP SHIPMENT: A shipment directly from the manufacturer to the end user.

EMPLOYER IDENTIFICATION NUMBER (EIN): A number obtained by a business from the IRS by filing form SS-4. If you are a sole proprietorship, your EIN is your Social Security number.

ENTREPRENEUR: Someone who is willing to assume the responsibility, risk and rewards of starting and operating a business.

EQUITY FINANCING: This involves "selling" a portion of your company to an outside investor. You have no obligation to repay the funds. In general, venture capital firms provide this type of funding.

FIDUCIARY: A person or company who holds a legal or ethical relationship of trust with one or more other parties (person or group of persons). Typically, a fiduciary prudently takes care of funds entrusted to it for safekeeping or investment.

FISCAL YEAR: Any 12-month period used by a company or government as an accounting period.

FIXED COST: A production cost which does not vary significantly with the volume of output. An example would be administrative costs. (Also see VARIABLE COST}.

FRANCHISE: A franchise is a form of licensing. The franchiser provides his services through a series of franchisees. Before investing in any franchise, check with the International Franchise Association at 1-800-543-1038 to see if the franchise is a member in good standing.

BUSINESS GLOSSARY

GRACE PERIOD: Time allowed a debtor in which legal action will not be undertaken by the creditor when payment is late.

LIEN: Legal right to hold property of another party or to have it sold or applied in payment of a claim.

LIQUIDATION: Sale of the assets of a business to pay off debts.

MARGINAL COST: Additional cost associated with producing one more unit of output.

OVERHEAD: Business expenses not directly related to a particular good or service produced. An example would be utilities.

POWER OF ATTORNEY: An agreement authorizing someone (generally an attorney) to act as your agent. This agreement may be general (complete authority) or special (limited authority).

PROFIT & LOSS (P & L) STATEMENT: A listing of income, expenses, and the resulting net profit or loss.

SBC (Small Business Centers): These 12 GSA centers located throughout the United States can help you tap the multi-billion-dollar GSA "market" for goods and services.

SBDC: Small Business Development Centers are located throughout the United States and are administered by the Small Business Association (SBA). They provide management assistance to entrepreneurs and new business owners.

SBIC (Small Business Investment Corporation): SBICs are licensed by the SBA as federally funded private venture capital firms. Money is available to small businesses under a variety of agreements.

SCORE: The Service Corps of Retired Executives is a volunteer management assistance program of the SBA. SCORE volunteers provide one-on-one counseling and workshops and seminars for small businesses. There are hundreds of SCORE offices throughout the United States.

SIMPLE INTEREST: Interest paid only on the principal of a loan.

BUSINESS GLOSSARY

SOLE PROPRIETORSHIP: The simplest (and most popular) form of business organization. The individual is personally liable for all debts of the business to the full extent of his or her property. On the other hand, the owner has complete control of the business.

SWEAT EQUITY: A common form of "investment." This refers to the investment in time that owners make, with no salary, to a new business.

TRIPLE NET: Rental type in which the tenant pays rent to the landlord and additionally assumes all costs regarding the operation, taxes and maintenance of the premises and building.

VARIABLE COST: Any costs which change significantly with the level of output. The obvious example is the cost of materials.

VENTURE CAPITAL: Money used to support new or unusual undertakings; equity, risk or speculative investment capital. This funding is provided to new or existing firms which exhibit potential for above-average growth.

DEBIT VS. CREDIT

Many people around the world choose to use banks as a way to hold their money. There are large national banks as well as smaller local banks. One of the main benefits to using a bank is the convenience of not having to carry cash with you. It is also a good way to track your spending thanks to online banking websites and apps. Those who have a bank account, will usually open both a checking account and a savings account.

A **checking account** is considered your main account. It is a place where you put most of your money or funds. You can choose to have your paychecks sent to your bank automatically though **direct deposit** or you can take cash directly to an ATM or bank teller and have it put into your account. Checking accounts are used to make purchases and pay bills. They also come with a **debit card**. A debit card is a plastic card that can be used online and in stores to make a purchase without carrying coins and cash. In order to use a debit card, the user will have to set up a **PIN** number. A PIN number is usually a four digit number that has to be entered for each purchase in order for the card to work. It helps protect against theft and fraud. That way, if you loose your card and someone else finds it, they won't be able to use it unless they know your specific PIN number. Many account holders also receive **checks**, which is another way to pay or send money to a person or company. When the person or company receives your check, they can deposit that amount into their own bank account.

A **savings account** is similar to a checking account, but it is not used for spending. It is a place where you can put money to save it for later. Some people have savings accounts for **short term goals**, like saving for a vacation or a new car. Others may open a savings account for **long term goals**, like saving for retirement or an emergency. Savings accounts usually allow you to make money off **interest**, which means the more money you save, the more money your bank will add to your account. Sometimes your bank may give you an ATM or debit card for your savings accounts, but they will usually limit the amount of times your can take money out. Remember, the goal of a savings account is to see how much money you can put into it, not how much you can spend.

Credit cards are much different than debit cards. When you use a credit card, you are borrowing money that isn't yours with the promise to pay it back. You are given a **credit limit**, which is a set amount of money on your card that you can borrow. You will get a statement, or bill, each month with the option to make a **minimum payment** or to pay off what you borrowed in full. Credit cards can be helpful when you need to make a purchase, but do not have enough in your checking or savings account to pay for it. However, you have to be very careful. Unlike checking and savings accounts where you can *make* extra money through interest, with a credit card, you will have to *pay* extra in **interest fees**.

Credit card holders also have the convenience of not having to carry cash and are usually better protected against theft and fraud since the money is owned by the bank. A lot of credit card companies also offer **rewards** to their cards, such as cash back or points. For example, if your credit card company offers 5% cash back, that means every time you spend $100 they will give you $5 back. Credit cards also help build your credit history and if used responsibly, can improve your credit score. A **credit score** is a number between 300-850 that is used to represent how responsible you are with finances and how likely you are to pay bills on time. Having a good credit score will allow you to have higher credit limits. It also provides you with more options if you choose to get a loan for a larger purchase, like buying a house or car. The higher your score, the less risk you are to the banks.

INTEREST

WHAT IS INTEREST? When you use a credit card you are using borrowed money. Why do banks want you to borrow money? So they can make money off interest. If you do not pay back the money you borrowed in full, then you will be charged an interest fee. Most credit card interest fees, also known as the APR, is usually around 15-27 percent. The longer it takes you to pay back the money, the more money you will pay in interest over time.

There are different types of interest: Fixed, Variable, Simple, Compound and Prime. Each method can be calculated differently. For this lesson we are going to focus on simple interest.

DIRECTIONS: Read the questions below and calculate the amount of interest that would be charged for each purchase. Then calculate the total cost of the item.

Dashawn buys a plane ticket to Montana. The plane ticket costs $382. His interest is 15% which is equal to $57. If he agrees to pay back the money within 2 years, how much will the ticket really cost?

	$57	YEARLY INTEREST		$382	COST OF ITEM
x	2	NUMBER OF YEARS IT TAKES TO PAYOFF	+	114	TOTAL INTEREST
	$114	TOTAL INTEREST		$496	TOTAL COST

Mariana wants to pay for her college tuition. The tuition costs $4,697 for the year. Her interest is 8% which is equal to $375.76. If she agrees to pay back the money within 5 years, how much will the tuition really cost?

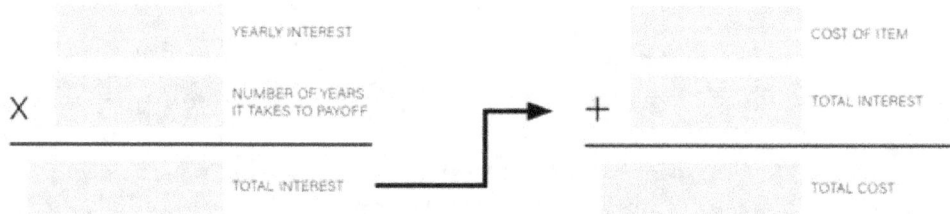

		YEARLY INTEREST			COST OF ITEM
X		NUMBER OF YEARS IT TAKES TO PAYOFF	+		TOTAL INTEREST
		TOTAL INTEREST			TOTAL COST

Olivia wants to pay for a new guitar. The guitar costs $1,999. Her interest is 28% which is equal to $559.72. If she agrees to pay back the money within 1 year, how much will the guitar really cost?

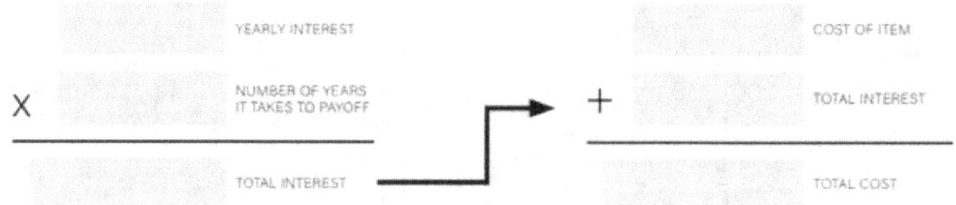

		YEARLY INTEREST			COST OF ITEM
X		NUMBER OF YEARS IT TAKES TO PAYOFF	+		TOTAL INTEREST
		TOTAL INTEREST			TOTAL COST

INTEREST

Fatima wants to buy a new car. The car costs $16,500. Her interest is 12% which is equal to $1980. If she agrees to pay back the money within 3 years, how much will the car really cost?

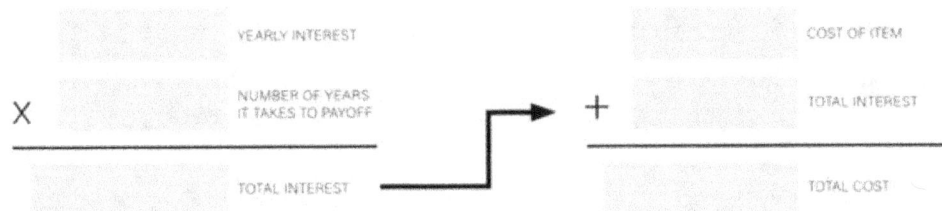

YEARLY INTEREST	COST OF ITEM
NUMBER OF YEARS IT TAKES TO PAYOFF	TOTAL INTEREST
TOTAL INTEREST	TOTAL COST

Chen wants to go on a cruise. The cruise costs $600. His interest is 3% which is equal to $18. If he agrees to pay back the money within 6 years, how much will the cruise really cost?

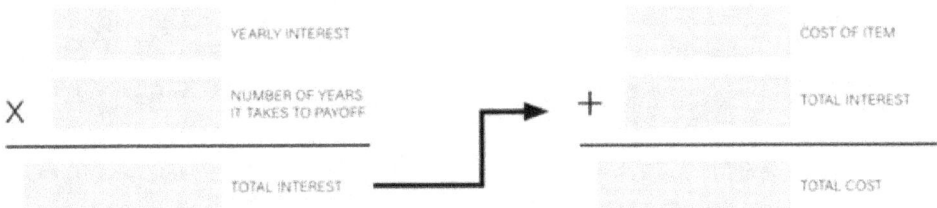

YEARLY INTEREST	COST OF ITEM
NUMBER OF YEARS IT TAKES TO PAYOFF	TOTAL INTEREST
TOTAL INTEREST	TOTAL COST

David wants to buy a gift. The gift costs $175.99. His interest is 17% which is equal to $29.92. If he agrees to pay back the money within 1 year, how much will the gift really cost?

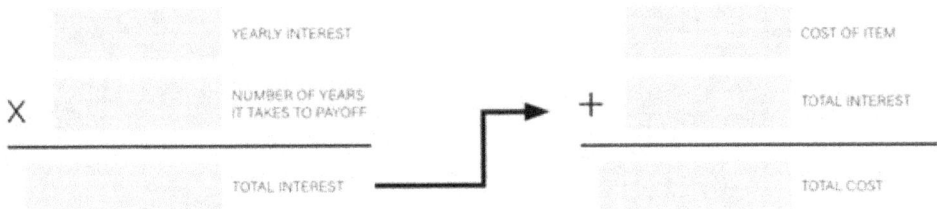

YEARLY INTEREST	COST OF ITEM
NUMBER OF YEARS IT TAKES TO PAYOFF	TOTAL INTEREST
TOTAL INTEREST	TOTAL COST

Tyrell wants to buy a wedding ring. The ring costs $3,200. His interest is 5% which is equal to $160. If he agrees to pay back the money within 8 years, how much will the ring really cost?

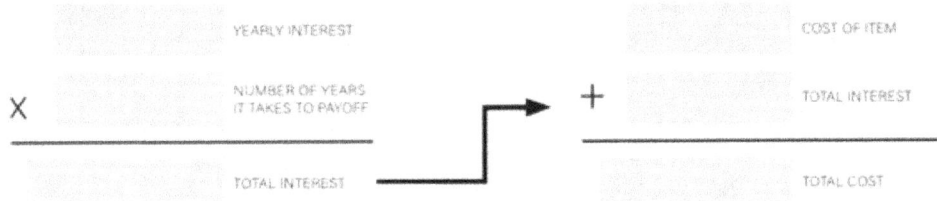

YEARLY INTEREST	COST OF ITEM
NUMBER OF YEARS IT TAKES TO PAYOFF	TOTAL INTEREST
TOTAL INTEREST	TOTAL COST

OVERDRAFT FEE

WHAT IS AN OVERDRAFT FEE? When you use a checking or debit account, you use your own money that you currently have in the bank. If you try to make a purchase and you don't have enough in your account you may get a decline, which means you will not be able to buy the item. However, in some situations, the purchase may go through even though you don't have enough money in your account. When that happens your bank may charge you an extra fee called and overdraft fee. An overdraft fee can be $20, $30 or another amount the bank chooses. It is a good idea to budget and keep a record of your spending so that you do not have to pay extra fees.

DIRECTIONS: Read the questions below and decide if there is enough money in your account to cover the purchase without being charged an overdraft fee. Circle your answer.

YES / NO There is $259.55 in your checking account. You need to pay your car payment, which is $309.22. Do you have enough money in your account to cover the cost without getting charged an overdraft fee?

YES / NO There is $952.47 in your checking account. You need to pay your rent, which is $800. Do you have enough money in your account to cover the cost without getting charged an overdraft fee?

YES / NO There is $350.11 in your checking account. You need to pay for groceries, which is $145.34. Do you have enough money in your account to cover the cost without getting charged an overdraft fee?

YES / NO There is $50.67 in your checking account. You need to pay for gas which is $20. Do you have enough money in your account to cover the cost without getting charged an overdraft fee?

YES / NO There is $517.19 in your checking account. You need to pay your electric bill, which is $213.99. Do you have enough money in your account to cover the cost without getting charged an overdraft fee?

YES / NO There is $400.01 in your checking account. You need to pay for a hotel stay, which is $609.55. Do you have enough money in your account to cover the cost without getting charged an overdraft fee?

YES / NO There is $163.28 in your checking account. You need to pay your phone bill which is $163.78. Do you have enough money in your account to cover the cost without getting charged an overdraft fee?

YES / NO There is $12.75 in your checking account. You need to pay for lunch, which is $8.99. Do you have enough money in your account to cover the cost without getting charged an overdraft fee?

Page 1 / 2
Education Credit Card | card ending in 0099
Apr 12, 2021 - May 12, 2021 | 31 days in billing cycle

Payment Information

Payment Due Date	**Jun 06, 2021**

Balance	Minimum Payment
$2,011.80	**$46.00**

If we do not receive your minimum payment by 8:00pm on the due date there is a late fee of $40.00

Rewards Summary

Rewards Balance	**$75.36**

Rewards can be redeemed for checks, gift cards and account credits. Go online for more details.

Account Summary

Previous Balance	$1,006.99
Payments	- $1,006.99
Transactions	+ $2,011.80
Cash Advance	+ $0.00
Fees Charges	+ $0.00
Interest Charged	+ $0.00
New Balance	**= $2,011.80**
Credit Limit	$4,500.00
Available Credit	$ 2,488.20

Transactions

LITTLE CARDHOLDER #0099

Transaction Date	Post Date	Description	Amount
Apr 17	Apr 19	Home Depot #2256	$1,675.23
Apr 27	Apr 28	Walmart #3478	$297.65
May 2	May 5	WaWa Gas Station #1119	$38.92
Total Transactions			**$2,011.80**

Interested Charged

Interest charge on purchases (last statement)	$0.00
Interest charge on cash advances	$0.00
Total Interest	$0.00

Your APR is 20.99% for purchases

- -

Pay or manage your account at www.educationbank.com

Customer Service 1-800-EDU-BANK

Payment Due Date: Jun 06, 2021

New Balance	Minimum Payment	Amount Enclosed
$2011.80	$46.00	$ _____

Please send this part of your statement along with a check to Education Credit. To ensure your payment is received on time allow at least 7 days for delivery.

Send Payments To:
Education Credit
123 LEARN AVENUE
BANKS, ALABAMA 36005

READING A STATEMENT

WHAT IS A STATEMENT? A statement is a monthly document that shows important information about your credit card or bank account. On a credit card statement you can see your interest charges, due date, minimum payment, rewards, balance, credit limit and APR. Bank account statements show your deposits (money you put into your account), transfers, interest earned, routing and account number and any overdraft fees. Both credit and debit accounts show your transactions for that month and any terms and conditions. It is a good idea to look over your monthly statements to make sure all the charges are correct and there are no fraudulent charges.

DIRECTIONS: Use the printed credit card statement to answer the questions. Then fill out a blank check for at LEAST the minimum amount due.

What is the last 4 digits of the card number? _____

When is the payment due by? _____

What is the minimum payment due? _____

What will happen if you make a payment on June 6th at 9:00pm?

_____

How much rewards cash is available? _____

Why was there no interest charged on the last statement?

_____

What is the previous balance? _____

What is the credit limit? _____

How much credit is available to spend? _____

How much was spent at WaWa Gas Station? _____

When did the Home Depot charge post? _____

Whats is the APR? _____

Where can you go manage the account? _____

Based on the information given, when would be a good day to send in your payment by mail?

_____

How much does Education Credit charge for a late fee? _____

What is the current balance? _____

PARTS OF A CARD

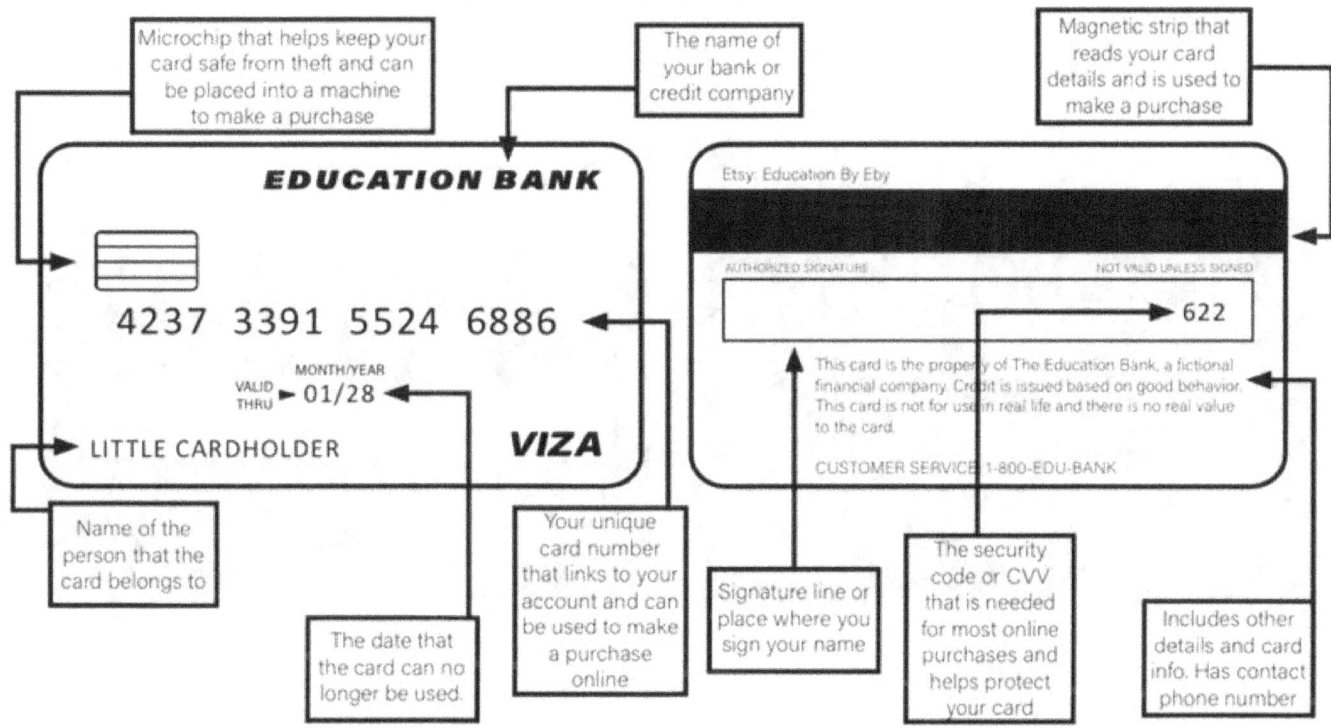

Microchip that helps keep your card safe from theft and can be placed into a machine to make a purchase

The name of your bank or credit company

Magnetic strip that reads your card details and is used to make a purchase

EDUCATION BANK

4237 3391 5524 6886

MONTH/YEAR
VALID THRU ► 01/28

LITTLE CARDHOLDER

VIZA

Etsy: Education By Eby

AUTHORIZED SIGNATURE   NOT VALID UNLESS SIGNED

622

This card is the property of The Education Bank, a fictional financial company. Credit is issued based on good behavior. This card is not for use in real life and there is no real value to the card.

CUSTOMER SERVICE: 1-800-EDU-BANK

Name of the person that the card belongs to

Your unique card number that links to your account and can be used to make a purchase online

The date that the card can no longer be used.

Signature line or place where you sign your name

The security code or CVV that is needed for most online purchases and helps protect your card

Includes other details and card info. Has contact phone number

DIRECTIONS: Print out this page. Then cut out the front and backs of the debit and credit cards below. Color them and sign your name on the signature line. Place the blank sides of the front and back of the cards together and laminate for more durability if using for pretend play.

EDUCATION BANK

4237 3391 5524 6886

MONTH/YEAR
VALID THRU ► 01/28

LITTLE CARDHOLDER

VIZA

Etsy: Education By Eby

AUTHORIZED SIGNATURE   NOT VALID UNLESS SIGNED

622

This card is the property of The Education Bank, a fictional financial company. Credit is issued based on good behavior. This card is not for use in real life and there is no real value to the card.

CUSTOMER SERVICE: 1-800-EDU-BANK

EDUCATION CREDIT

9987 6544 3211 0099

MONTH/YEAR
VALID THRU ► 07/28

LITTLE CARDHOLDER

Etsy: Education By Eby

AUTHORIZED SIGNATURE   NOT VALID UNLESS SIGNED

832

This card is the property of The Education Bank, a fictional financial company. Credit is issued based on good behavior. This card is not for use in real life and there is no real value to the card.

CUSTOMER SERVICE: 1-800-EDU-BANK

EDUCATION BANK

4237 3391 5524 6886

MONTH/YEAR
VALID
THRU ► 01/28

LITTLE CARDHOLDER

VIZA

Etsy: Education By Eby

AUTHORIZED SIGNATURE   NOT VALID UNLESS SIGNED

622

This card is the property of The Education Bank, a fictional
financial company. Credit is issued based on good behavior.
This card is not for use in real life and there is no real value
to the card.

CUSTOMER SERVICE: 1-800-EDU-BANK

EDUCATION CREDIT

9987 6544 3211 0099

MONTH/YEAR
VALID
THRU ► 07/28

LITTLE CARDHOLDER

Etsy: Education By Eby

AUTHORIZED SIGNATURE   NOT VALID UNLESS SIGNED

832

This card is the property of The Education Bank, a fictional
financial company. Credit is issued based on good behavior.
This card is not for use in real life and there is no real value
to the card.

CUSTOMER SERVICE: 1-800-EDU-BANK

CHECK REGISTERS

Take a look at the transactions and input them in the Check Register below. Remember: When $ comes out of your account, it goes in the "Withdrawl" column. When $ comes in, it goes in the "Deposit" column. Your "Opening Balance" is the amount of money you have in your account before the transactions come in/out. Don't forget to record your balance at the end of each row. Use an additional sheet to calculate the balances, if you need to.

TRANSACTIONS

1. On January 5th, you received $20 in the mail from your Grandma for your birthday. You brought it to the bank that same day.

2. On January 10th, you spent $10 at McDonald's for lunch.

3. On January 25th, you spent $5 at "Billy Bob's Cards" on trading cards.

4. On January 30th, you wrote a check for $15 for Girl Scout cookies.

CHECK REGISTER				
DATE	TRANSACTION	WITHDRAWL	DEPOSIT	BALANCE
Jan. 1	OPENING BALANCE			$100

Do you have enough money left over in your account to pay back your brother the $20 that you borrowed? _____

PRACTICE WRITING CHECKS

Fill in the information for the checks below.

1. $55.38 for Target

```
Your Name
Your Street Address                                           1025
Your City, State, and Zip Code
Your Phone Number
                                        DATE _____

PAY TO THE
ORDER OF _____  $ _____

_____ DOLLARS 🔒 Security Features
                                                        Included
                                                        Details on Back

MEMO _____          _____
⑆000000000⑆ ⑆000000000⑆        ⑈1025
```

2. $1,000,0000 for your best friend

```
Your Name
Your Street Address                                           1026
Your City, State, and Zip Code
Your Phone Number
                                        DATE _____

PAY TO THE
ORDER OF _____  $ _____

_____ DOLLARS 🔒 Security Features
                                                        Included
                                                        Details on Back

MEMO _____          _____
⑆000000000⑆ ⑆000000000⑆        ⑈1026
```

DANGERS OF CREDIT CARD DEBT

WHAT IS DEBT? "Debt" is simply, money that you owe.

WHAT IS A CREDIT CARD? A credit card is a small plastic card that you can use to pay for things by borrowing money from a bank or business.

IS USING A CREDIT CARD FREE? No! If you don't pay the credit card company back within the first 30 days, they will charge you money (known as "interest") every single month until it is paid off.

EXAMPLE: If you buy a bike for $300 with a credit card, you could end up paying almost $90 in interest over the course of a year!

+ $90 interest

= $390!

NOTE: Credit cards have all different interest rates. Some are more. Some are less. Some credit card companies even charge an extra fee every year just for having the card!

THINK ABOUT IT! What would be a better way to pay for the bike without having to put it on a credit card?

_____

_____

_____

CALCULATE IT! How much money is wasted on paying interest in the examples below?

$570 Total paid to credit card
- $475 **LAP TOP**
_____
INTEREST PAID

$350 Total paid to credit card
- $280 **BASKETBALL STANDARD**
_____
INTEREST PAID

$122 Total paid to credit card
- $100 **SHOES**
_____
INTEREST PAID

$475 Total paid to credit card
- $405 **GAMING SYSTEM**
_____
INTEREST PAID

PRIORITIZING

NEED = something you need to survive.

WANT = something you don't need to survive, but would like.

It's important to **PRIORITIZE!** When planning out how you will spend your money, you first must decide what your **"NEEDS"** are and what your **"WANTS"** are, and make sure to **PAY FOR YOUR NEEDS FIRST!**

List 5 examples of "Needs" and 5 examples of "Wants"

NEEDS

1. _____

2. _____

3. _____

4. _____

5. _____

WANTS

1. _____

2. _____

3. _____

4. _____

5. _____

If you were trying to save money, what 3 things would you choose NOT to buy for awhile?

1. _____

2. _____

3. _____

PLAN YOUR SPENDING

Take a look at the budgets below. Select only the "NEEDS" from the list of expenses and write each one in the table. Add up the total ,and make sure that it is LESS than your weekly budget.

BUDGET:$350

EXPENSES:

$130 Water Bill

$50 Eating out at Restaurant

$100 Groceries

$35 Movie Tickets

$85 Electric Bill

NEED	$ AMOUNT
TOTAL =	

Total must be less than $350

BUDGET:$1600

EXPENSES:

$1500 Mortgage Payment

$80 Gas Bill

$250 New Clothes

$75 Tickets to Basketball Game

$25 Comic Books

NEED	$ AMOUNT
TOTAL =	

Total must be less than $1600

BUDGET:$150

EXPENSES:

$75 Medicine

$150 Concert Tickets

$40 Gas for Car

$35 Hygiene Items (Soap, etc.)

$25 Ice Cream

NEED	$ AMOUNT
TOTAL =	

Total must be less than $150

GIVE, SAVE, SPEND

DID YOU KNOW THAT YOU CAN START BUDGETING YOUR MONEY NOW? It's true! Budgeting money is such a valuable habit and skill to learn! The sooner you start, the better off you'll be.

While you're young, your budget is simple. In fact, it only needs to have three categories: GIVE, SAVE, AND SPEND.

Remember: you need to: PLAN FIRST, SPEND LATER

By learning how to set goals and make decisions about your money, you are preparing yourself for success now and in the future.

Take a look at the categories below, and list 3 reasons for putting money into each one. For example: Who would you like to **GIVE** *your money to? What would you like to* **SPEND** *your money on now? What would you like* **SAVE** *up to buy later?*

1. _____

2. _____

3. _____

1. _____

2. _____

3. _____

1. _____

2. _____

3. _____

HOMEWORK ASSIGNMENT: *Create 3 containers for budgeting your money, labeled "Give, Save, and Spend." It could be as simple as three envelopes, or as fancy an hand-made, decorated boxes.*

NEEDS VS. WANTS

WHAT HAPPENS IF YOU SPEND MORE MONEY THAN YOU MAKE? Well, eventually, you go broke. And, who wants that? Nobody. So what can you do? **DON'T SPEND ALL YOUR MONEY!** Simple as that! Well, sometimes that's easier said than done, but a great place to start is by looking at what you spend (or want to spend) your money on, and asking yourself: **IS THIS SOMETHING I** <u>NEED</u> **OR SOMETHING I** <u>WANT</u>? *A "need" is something you can't live without, and a "want" is something you'd like to have to make your life more enjoyable.* And, sometimes we can't always have everything we want. Sorry! When planning how you are going to spend your money, it's important to know how to separate your needs from your wants. You want to make sure you have enough to **COVER YOUR NEEDS FIRST** before spending any money on things you want.

Take a look at the items below and decide whether you think each one is a NEED or a WANT.

Color the WANTS yellow and the NEEDS green.

BASIC FOOD	CELL PHONE	SHAMPOO	ARCADE TOKENS
VIDEO GAMES	SHELTER	TOYS	
WATER	CAR	NEW BICYCLE	COMIC BOOKS
VACATIONS	SOAP	EATING OUT 5 TIMES A WEEK	CANDY
MEDICINE	MANSION	DESIGNER CLOTHES	
CONCERT TICKETS	BASIC CLOTHES	TOOTHPASTE	

ARE THERE MORE NEEDS OR MORE WANTS? _____

IF YOU WERE TRYING TO SAVE MONEY, WHAT ARE 3 OF YOUR 'WANTS' YOU COULD GO WITHOUT FOR

AWHILE? _____

STAYING WITHIN A BUDGET

WHAT IS A BUDGET? To put it simply, a budget is how you plan to spend your money, while not going over a certain amount. Why might it be important to create a budget (or plan)?

CREATE YOUR OWN BUDGETS! Look at the _average_ cost of items, listed at the top of each budget below. Fill in your own amounts in each table. You may choose to spend more, less, or the same amount as the average, but your total amount at the bottom CANNOT be higher than the total you have to spend (you may need a calculator).

MY "BACK-TO-SCHOOL SHOPPING" BUDGET

AVERAGE COSTS = $270

Clothes – $150
Shoes – $50
Backpack– $30
Lunchbox – $15
Classroom Supplies – $25

TOTAL YOU HAVE TO SPEND = $250

ITEM	AMOUNT
Clothes	
Shoes	
Backpack	
Lunchbox	
Classroom Supplies	
TOTAL =	

WHERE DID YOU SAVE MONEY AND HOW?

LEFT OVER $? WHAT WOULD YOU DO WITH IT?

MY "BIRTHDAY PARTY" BUDGET

AVERAGE COSTS = $570

Bounce House – $250
Food – $100
Decorations – $50
Presents – $100
Goody Bags – $60
Invitations – $10

TOTAL YOU HAVE TO SPEND = $500

ITEM	AMOUNT
Bounce House	
Food	
Decorations	
Presents	
Goody Bags	
Invitations	
TOTAL =	

WHERE DID YOU SAVE MONEY AND HOW?

LEFT OVER $? WHAT WOULD YOU DO WITH IT?

CREATE A HOUSEHOLD BUDGET

THINK ABOUT THE FUTURE! What kind of lifestyle would you like? Did you know it costs money to run a household? Pretend you are a responsible adult and select which items you'd like to include in your monthly budget and how much you'd like to spend. These prices are just ideas, based on the average household budget in the U.S. You don't have to include every option, and feel free to add some of your own ideas! It's your choice!

HEADS UP! This list does not cover every possible expense. For some expenses, you have less of a choice (such as taxes, insurance, and unexpected costs). Today, we'll just work with the options that you'll have more control over.

NOTE TO PARENTS: Talk to your child about the effects of selecting a more expensive option and a less expensive option.

SELECT ITEMS FROM THIS LIST TO INCLUDE IN YOUR MONTHLY BUDGET

Mortgage/Rent: $500 – $3,000+

Savings: $0 – $5,000+

Groceries: $300 – $800+

Car: $0 – $1000+

Vacations: $0 – $2000+

Lessons: $0 – $800+

Electricity: $50 – $500+

Eating Out: $0 – $400+

Charity: $0 – $5,000+

Gifts: $0 – $1,000+

Household Products: $50 – $350+

Entertainment: $0 – $500+

Cell Phones: $0 – $400+

Clothes: $10 – $1,000+

Haircuts: $0 – $100+

Water: $25 – $200+

House Phone: $0 – $50+

Internet: $0 – $75+

Pets: $0 – $250+

MY FUTURE MONTHLY BUDGET

ITEM	COST	ITEM	COST
	$		$
	$		$
	$		$
	$		$
	$		$
	$		$
	$		$
	$		$
	$		$
	$		$
	$		$

MONTHLY TOTAL (add all yellow boxes) **=**

WHAT WOULD IT COST YOU PER YEAR?
(multiply your monthly total by 12)

_____

AVERAGE YEARLY HOUSEHOLD INCOME: $59,000

MEET ZOE'

When the world shut down during the COVID-19 pandemic and community libraries closed their doors, Zoe Howlett saw a need and decided to act. She knew that many children didn't have books at home some didn't even have library cards. Wanting to make a difference, Zoe purchased and donated 6,000 books, giving hundreds of families a week's worth of reading adventures.

Through her generosity, Zoe helped bridge the gap for kids who might have otherwise gone without stories, learning, and imagination during a difficult time. Her mission was simple: to make sure every child could experience the magic of books, even when the world outside felt uncertain. In doing so, Zoe not only filled homes with books she filled hearts with hope.